INFLUENTIAL
L!VES

SHONDA RHIMES

TV PRODUCER, SCREENWRITER, AND SHOWRUNNER

Naida Redgrave

Published in 2018 by Enslow Publishing, LLC.
101 W. 23rd Street, Suite 240, New York, NY 10011

Library of Congress Cataloging-in-Publication Data

Names: Redgrave, Naida author.
Title: Shonda Rhimes : tv producer, screenwriter, and showrunner / Naida Redgrave.
Description: New York : Enslow Publishing, 2018. | Series: Influential lives | Includes bibliographical references and index. Audience: Grades 6-12.
Identifiers: LCCN 2017003077 | ISBN 9780766085039 (library-bound)
Subjects: LCSH: Rhimes, Shonda--Juvenile literature. | Women television producers and directors--United States--Biography--Juvenile literature. | African American television producers and directors--Biography--Juvenile literature. | African American women screenwriters Juvenile literature.--Biography
Classification: LCC PN1992.4.R515 Z75 2017 | DDC 791.4502/32--dc23
LC record available at https://lccn.loc.gov/2017003077

Printed in the United States of America

To Our Readers: We have done our best to make sure all websites in this book were active and appropriate when we went to press. However, the author and the publisher have no control over and assume no liability for the material available on those websites or on any websites they may link to. Any comments or suggestions can be sent by e-mail to customerservice@enslow.com.

Photo credits: Cover, p. 1 Helga Esteb/Shutterstock.com; p. 4 Stefanie Keenan/Getty Images; p. 8 Marla Aufmuth/Getty Images; p. 14 Jason LaVeris/FilmMagic; p. 19 Steve Granitz/WireImage/Getty Images; p. 23 Lee Snider/Corbis/Getty Images; p. 25 Nancy R. Schiff/Hulton Archive/Getty Images; pp. 30–31, 48–49 Photos 12/Alamy Stock Photo; p. 34 Archive Photos/Moviepix/Getty Images; p. 38 Gilbert Carrasquillo/FilmMagic/Getty Images; p. 42 Michael Tran/FilmMagic/Getty Images; p. 44 Earl Gibson III/Getty Images; pp. 54–55 Kevin Winter/Getty Images; p. 57 Jordan Strauss /Invision/AP; pp. 62–63 Bryan Bedder/Getty Images; pp. 66–67 REUTERS/Alamy Stock Photo; pp. 68–69 ZUMA Press, Inc./Alamy Stock Photo; pp. 74–75 Alberto E. Rodriguez/Getty Images; p. 78 Paul Zimmerman/Getty Images; pp. 80–81 Paul Zimmerman/Getty Images; pp. 84–85 Bettmann/Getty Images; p. 87 WENN Ltd/Alamy Stock Photo; pp. 90–91 Tony Barson/FilmMagic /Getty Images; pp. 96–97 Gilbert Carrasquillo/Getty Images; p. 98 Nicholas Hunt/Getty Images; p. 100 Everett Collection Inc/Alamy Stock Photo; back cover and interior pages background graphic zffoto/Shutterstock.com.

Contents

CHAPTER ONE

"What Am I Afraid They Will See?"

O n June 8, 2014, when Shonda Rhimes walked onto the stage and took her position at the podium at Dartmouth College, she took a deep breath into the microphone.[1] Today, she was giving a commencement speech, a speech delivered to students when they graduate university. Dartmouth is Rhimes's *alma mater*, a Latin phrase that means a school that a person previously attended. In 1991, twenty-three years earlier, Shonda had been sitting patiently, just like the students she could see in front of her. She had worn the same green cap and gown, just like these students, and awaited the commencement speech. In 1991, the speaker had been Elizabeth Dole, a politician and president of the American Red Cross (a charitable organization that provides emergency assistance, relief, and education in the United States).

With several hit television shows and Hollywood clout, Shonda Rhimes is the epitome of success. Still, it has taken her years to embrace the opportunities that come with that success.

On this day in June 2014, however, Rhimes was not a college student waiting to be inspired by the words of an esteemed person. Instead, she was about to give the prestigious commencement speech in front of sixteen thousand people, and the thought of it terrified her. At that point, the writer, producer, and showrunner had already been responsible for four television shows; *Grey's Anatomy*, *Private Practice*, *Off the Map*, and *Scandal*. Just around the corner was *How to Get Away with Murder*, the show that, once aired, would cause Thursday nights on ABC to be known as "Shonda's Night." Three of Rhimes's shows would appear on the channel, back-to-back, elevating the Dartmouth graduate into one of the most powerful women in television.

The American Broadcasting Company (ABC)

The American Broadcasting Company (ABC) is a television network owned by a division of the Walt Disney Company. ABC has its headquarters in New York City and has additional offices in Los Angeles and Burbank, California. The company started as a radio broadcasting network but began making television shows in 1948. It was bought by Disney in 1995 and since then has been known for successful drama shows like *Lost, Desperate Housewives*, and *Grey's Anatomy*.[2]

All of this success didn't alleviate the fear Rhimes felt about giving the speech. In the weeks leading up to that moment, she was paralyzed with nerves. One morning while brushing her teeth and listening to NPR (National Public Radio), she heard someone on the show say that they were most looking forward to hearing her commencement speech over any others. Feeling an immense pressure weigh down on her, Rhimes sent a group email to her women's online network. It was two weeks before the commencement, and she had still not yet written a single word. For Rhimes, this was strange. Of all the things that Shonda Rhimes is good at, writing is at the top of the list.

As a little girl playing in her mother's pantry, she would make up characters and stories. As she got older, she found comfort in the stories she wrote. That love and passion for words never left her, through high school, then college, and then film school. Rhimes's strength was in her words—the power she invoked through them and the tales she wove with them. Rhimes is a writer to the core; this is what helped build her career and is what sustained it. And yet, on this occasion, two weeks before her speech at the college she used to attend, Rhimes could not write a word.

Rhimes was not just afraid of standing in front of sixteen thousand people (although that was a large part of it). She was also afraid that the speech would be filmed and uploaded online, where it would be available to millions of people. Despite being a born writer, Rhimes is also an introvert. Although she was a hugely successful writer and showrunner, up until this point, she had managed to avoid the public eye. She rarely agreed to

The first step of Rhimes's "Year of Yes" journey was agreeing to give the commencement speech at Dartmouth. Once she got up onstage and starting speaking from her heart, she discovered that she was no longer afraid.

• •

interviews and did not attend many industry parties or social gatherings unless she had to.

This year, however, was part of her "Year of Yes"—the year that Rhimes decided to say yes to more opportunities and force herself out of her comfort zone. The experiences would lead her to write a memoir, *Year of Yes*, about her adventure. The Dartmouth speech was one of the first times that Rhimes truly stepped out of her comfort zone

What Does a Showrunner Do?

The showrunner is usually one of the executive producers on a television show, whose job it is to oversee all of the scripts and writing staff. The showrunner is in charge of the development and story lines in every script. He or she is also responsible for putting together and maintaining the show bible, which has all of the information about every character and story line in the show. The showrunner manages the director and crew and has to make sure that the cast and crew work well together.[3]

and said yes to a challenging new experience. And there she was, two weeks before the event, terrified.

Rhimes sought advice from the women in her online network. One woman reminded her that, as long as she did not soil herself onstage, then she would be fine. It reassured Rhimes, as she knew that this was unlikely to happen. Despite her fear of being judged by hundreds of thousands of strangers, knowing that at least she wouldn't completely embarrass herself gave Rhimes the little push she needed to start writing her speech. She started small at first, writing little notes on scraps of paper and in her iPhone Notes app. Slowly but surely, her speech started to come together, but still, something didn't feel quite right.

Dartmouth College

One of the eight Ivy League universities in the US Northeast, Dartmouth College educates the cream of the crop in the liberal arts. Located in Hanover, New Hampshire, Dartmouth was founded in 1769. A very exclusive school, Dartmouth enrolls approximately forty-three hundred undergraduate students annually. The college also includes four small postgraduate institutions: a medical school, business school, graduate school, and engineering school.

Until 1972, when it finally began admitting women, Dartmouth was exclusively a men's college. Today, Dartmouth students can be certain they are the best of the best, as admissions standards are among the highest in the nation.

On the plane on the way to Dartmouth, Rhimes took a proper look at the whole speech. While reading it, she did not feel reassured or positive. Instead, she felt sick. Rhimes thought long and hard about what was wrong with it. It was well written, it had some jokes and moments of levity, and it was smart. It was exactly the type of thing she would normally write. Suddenly, she realized what was wrong. She wasn't revealing or sharing anything personal. She was using her voice, but she was not speaking from her heart. This troubled Rhimes. She realized that she had written the speech from a place of safety, of fear, being careful not to reveal too much of herself. She was too afraid that she might be judged negatively if she revealed herself. However, in not sharing her true self with the graduating students, she was not truly imparting her knowledge and wisdom to them. "What am I afraid they will see if I really am myself?" she asked herself, as she read through the speech four more times on the plane. Then and there, Rhimes decided to start the speech over.

Her new speech was more chatty, like she was having a conversation with a friend over coffee. Although it felt strange to be less formal, particularly for such a momentous occasion as the Dartmouth graduation, it was also a lot more honest. Finally, the speech sounded like her, and it was coming from her heart. Rhimes saved the document and enjoyed the rest of her flight. The next morning, she woke up in her hotel room before dawn and waited for the fear to set in. She was expecting it to hit her so badly that she wouldn't be able to give the speech. As the day went on and she accepted her honorary PhD, Rhimes was still waiting for the fear to take a hold of her. She waited right up to the very second that she walked up to the podium and stood in front of the microphone, looking out to the audience. Suddenly, she took a deep breath and realized something incredible—she was not afraid. Although she was up onstage, alone, in front of sixteen thousand people, the confidence she had in the honesty of her speech meant she was not afraid. Rhimes was, for the first

> **"What am I afraid they will see if I really am myself?"**

time in her life, speaking as herself to the world. And it gave her great strength.

Shonda Rhimes—who was once the introverted girl from suburban Chicago, who played in band and had "Coke-bottle-thick glasses"—was in her element. On June 8, 2014, after all the years of disappearing into her hard work, she found the confidence to stand in front of the world, without hiding, and speak honestly from her heart.[4]

CHAPTER TWO

Making Stuff Up

• •

Shonda Lynn Rhimes was born on January 13, 1970, in University Park, Chicago, Illinois.[1] At the time she was born, University Park was known as Park Forest South, and Richard Nixon was president of the United States.[2]

Rhimes is the youngest of six children. She has three older sisters, Delorse, Elnora, and Sandie, and two older brothers, James and Tony. There is a twelve-year age difference between Shonda and her eldest sister, Delorse. As a child, Delorse was Shonda's role model. As an adult, Shonda now sees Delorse as one of her best friends.[3]

Both of Rhimes's parents have an academic background. Her mother, Vera, worked as a university administrator, and her father, Ilee Rhimes Jr., worked as a college professor. While raising six children, her mother also attended college to earn a PhD. Her father, who has an MBA, was the chief information officer at the University of Southern California until 2013.

Rhimes is the youngest of six children. She was a very quiet and creative child who loved to read and make up stories. Her creative imagination later got her into trouble at school, as she would tell her classmates made-up stories about her life.

• •

Creative Beginnings

From a very young age, Vera Rhimes felt that Shonda showed signs of being very creative. When she was just three years old, rather than play with real toys, Shonda would ask to play in the pantry with the canned goods. In her book, *Year of Yes*, she recalls how much fun she had creating stories using the different cans of food. Although Rhimes describes having a wonderful childhood, she was always more comfortable in her imagination and making up stories than she was with real people.[4] From childhood and into adulthood, she was always an introvert, so she found more comfort in reading books than in real situations.

> "Making stuff up is responsible for everything I've done, everything I am, everything I have."

Growing up, Shonda shared a room with her sister Sandie. In her book, Rhimes shares family photos. She describes how she secretly hid books in the back of her underpants while the photos were taken. Once they were done, she found a hiding place to read alone. As a child, Shonda spent most of her time buried in books. She spent her evenings under her covers with a flashlight, reading scary novels by Stephen King. When she got too afraid, she would lock the book inside her closet, as she felt that the characters would not be able to get her from there.[5]

Being an introvert and enjoying making up stories sometimes got Rhimes into trouble, especially as a student at St. Mary's Catholic School in Park Forest, Illinois. When the nuns at the school caught her making up stories and not telling the truth, they made her recite the rosary over recess. One of the stories she made up at school was that her mother had escaped from Russia after trying to assassinate a man named Leonid Brezhnev. In real life, Brezhnev was the general secretary of the Soviet Union Communist Party from 1964 to 1982. In Shonda's made-up version, her mother had attempted to stop a nuclear war and save America, which is when she was forced to flee Russia, leaving behind her fiancé Vladimir.

The very thing that got her into trouble at school is what eventually made her successful. As Rhimes explained in her book, "Making stuff up is responsible

Reciting the Rosary

In Catholicism, reciting the rosary is a type of prayer that is performed with a set of rosary beads, which look similar to a necklace made of beads with a crucifix pendant. When reciting the prayers, a person holds the cross in the right hand while sliding beads across the chain with the other hand. Counting the beads helps free the mind, allowing the person to concentrate on praying. It is a way for people of the Catholic faith to meditate and pray in order to feel closer to God.

for everything I've done, everything I am, everything I have."[6]

Rhimes later attended Marian Catholic High School in Chicago Heights, Illinois, where she played the oboe in the school band. As of 2016, the Marian Catholic Band had won its class in the Illinois State marching band competition every year for thirty-six years, since 1980. In the Bands of America Competition, the band has been the Summer National Champion five times and Grand National Champion seven times.[7]

While in high school, Rhimes got her first first job at the ice cream parlor Baskin-Robbins, and she has had a job ever since. Some of the jobs have even influenced her television shows; her time spent as a candy striper gave her an interest in hospital environments, which

The Oboe

Shonda Rhimes played the oboe in her high school band. The oboe is a woodwind instrument that is held vertically and is shaped like a long tube that flares out at the end. The two-foot-long instrument is black with metal keys that are used to play different notes. To play it, the oboe is held upright and air is blown through the mouthpiece. The mouthpiece is a double reed. When air is blown into the reed, it vibrates, and this vibration causes the air inside of the oboe to move, which makes the instrument's sound. There are usually between two and four oboes in an orchestra.

became useful inspiration for her television show *Grey's Anatomy*.[8]

Growing Pains

As a teenager, Rhimes had thick glasses and barely spoke at school, preferring to spend her time reading. She did, however, have an unusual morning ritual. Each day, she put time and effort into trying to make her hair look like pop star Whitney Houston's. Using a curling iron and a bottle of hair spray to get the look, Shonda sometimes burned her fingers in the pursuit of perfection. She spent hours and hours over the years trying to perfect the hairstyle, believing that if her hair was flawless like Whitney Houston's, then her life would be, too. Much later, when she was living in Los Angeles after college, Rhimes found out that Whitney Houston's hairstyle had been a wig all along.[9]

Growing up, she was a big fan of *The Oprah Winfrey Show*, a talk show hosted by Oprah Winfrey, an American media mogul, talk show host, actress, producer, and philanthropist. [9] Rhimes took notes on the things Winfrey talked about and read all the books Winfrey suggested. Little did she know that one day, as she became more successful, she would be invited to appear on the show multiple times.

As a young girl, Rhimes also enjoyed watching real-life surgeries on television. Although a career in medicine seemed on the cards, one thing stood in the way—Shonda did not have an aptitude for science.[11] In an interview with CNN, she recalled a teacher from those early years who made her look forward to the

Oprah Winfrey's wildly influential talk show was an inspiration to Rhimes. Winfrey is credited with creating a new type of talk show, where people discussed their lives freely and emotionally.

future. Her fifth-grade teacher, Mrs. Hanks, had a youthful nature and the ability to make her students really care by making learning fun. "She was...one of the very few non-Nuns that I had been taught by and there was something about her that made me feel like growing up was going to be exciting." One day, while Shonda waited for her mom to collect her after school, Mrs. Hanks let her watch the television soap opera *General Hospital*. Rhimes still thinks about Mrs. Hanks to this day and wonders what happened to her. [12] By the time Shonda graduated from Marian Catholic High School in the class of 1987, she was looking forward to what the future would bring.

CHAPTER THREE

The Pursuit of Passion

• • • • • • • • • • • • • • • • •

After high school, Rhimes attended Dartmouth College, an Ivy League research university in Hanover, New Hampshire. While there, she majored in English and film studies, earning her bachelor's degree in 1991. During an interview with the *Hollywood Reporter*, Rhimes told the interviewer that the reason she chose English was because she had "no affinity for math and science whatsoever." At the time, she had dreams of becoming the next Toni Morrison, the Nobel Prize–winning American novelist. However, she changed her mind when she realized that she could not be exactly the same as her idol, and she did not want to be an imitation of somebody else.[1]

Rhimes loved being at Dartmouth. During her time there, she joined the Black Underground Theater Association (BUTA), where she directed and performed in a number of student productions. The BUTA is a theater group that develops work written, directed, and performed by people from diverse

Famous People Who Went to Dartmouth College

Dr. Seuss

Theodor Seuss Geisel was an American writer, cartoonist, and book publisher, best known for the popular children's books written under the pen name Dr. Seuss. These include *The Cat in the Hat*, *Green Eggs and Ham*, and *The Lorax*.

Mindy Kaling

Mindy Kaling, whose real name is Vera Mindy Chokalingam, is an American actress, comedian, writer, and producer. She is known for creating *The Mindy Project* and appearing in *Inside Out* and *The Office*.

Nelson Rockefeller

American businessman, philanthropist, public servant, and politician Nelson Aldrich Rockefeller served as the forty-first vice president of the United States under President Gerald Ford, and also as the forty-ninth governor of New York.

backgrounds.[2] Rhimes also wrote for the college newspaper, the *Dartmouth*, which was founded in 1799 and is America's oldest college newspaper.[3]

On her graduation day, while all of her friends were celebrating, Rhimes was grieving. When it was time to leave college, she lay on her dorm room floor crying while her mother packed up her things.[4] She knew that there was a long road ahead of her and

Dartmouth College ranks among the world's top academic institutions. During her time there, Rhimes directed and performed in theater productions and wrote for the college newspaper.

that road was in the real world, away from the safety and comfort of the familiar Dartmouth environment. Although she didn't know it at the time, Rhimes was destined to return to her beloved college once again, to deliver the commencement speech to its 2014 graduates.

Into the Real World

After graduating, Rhimes relocated to San Francisco to live with one of her siblings. Once there, she managed to secure a job at the advertising firm McCann Erickson.[5] The company had recently been tasked with putting together an advertising campaign for Barbie, the iconic doll. As part of the campaign, the firm asked employees to reflect on their childhood memories of playing with the doll. Rhimes wrote about playing with Barbie dolls when she was a young girl. McCann Erickson filmed a test commercial using Rhimes's story. She thought it was really cool to see her words performed out loud and realized she had a knack for writing. Rhimes was proving herself to be bright and capable in her job, but something was missing—she had no passion for advertising.

Around that time, she also continued to develop her love for television. As a child, she looked up to actresses of color who had achieved great success, such as Whoopi Goldberg, Phylicia Rashad, and Oprah Winfrey. Bothered by her lack of passion for advertising, Rhimes started to watch reruns of shows she loved, paying close attention to the writing. Then one day, when she was twenty-two years old, a

Rhimes felt inspired by the actresses of color she saw on television and in movies, such as Whoopi Goldberg. She decided on a career in show business after seeing a live broadcast of Goldberg performing on Broadway.

miraculous idea occurred to her.[6] Rhimes was reading a news article that claimed the USC (University of Southern California) School of Cinema-Television was harder to get into than Harvard Law School. Her competitive nature plus her desire for a creative challenge led her to apply. Rhimes was accepted, which triggered the next step of her journey to success.[7]

Grabbing the opportunity by the horns, Rhimes's intuitive writing ability, along with her hard work and determination, took her to the top of her class. During this time, she caught the eye of Debra Martin Chase, a high-flying producer. Chase took Rhimes under her wing, hiring her as an intern at Mundy Lane, a production company owned by the Oscar-winning

USC Cinematic Arts

The USC School of Cinematic Arts (formerly the USC School of Cinema-Television) is a private film school within the University of Southern California, Los Angeles. Established in 1929, it is the largest and oldest film school in the United States. USC often ranks as the best film program in the world and is considered harder to get into than Harvard Law School.[8] Once students are accepted they knuckle down to some hard work. Students at the school produce around 230 hours of motion pictures and more than one hundred screenplays each year.[9]

actor Denzel Washington. Chase's experience in the industry placed Rhimes in a prime position to launch her career.[10] To this day, Rhimes credits Chase for mentoring her toward her early success.[11]

While pursuing her master of fine arts (MFA) at the University of Southern California, Rhimes was awarded the Gary Rosenberg Writing Fellowship, which came with a $10,000 cash prize. The fellowship furthered her reputation as an excellent screenwriter, and when she graduated in 1994, she already had an agent in place.[12]

CHAPTER FOUR

The House That Britney Built

· · · · · · · · · · · · · · · · · · ·

Thanks to the Gary Rosenberg Writing Fellowship, Shonda Rhimes's name was soon known in the right circles. And armed with an impressive thesis script, the future looked bright. Success, however, came slowly. To make ends meet, she took on a number of different jobs. She worked as an office administrator, and then became a counselor at a center that taught job skills to homeless people.[1] This felt like a sidestep to Rhimes, who was eager to get her career off the ground. In a moment of doubt, she briefly considered medical school, but before long she was offered a research director job on the HBO documentary *Hank Aaron: Chasing the Dream*. The documentary won a Peabody Award in 1995.[2]

A Way In

In 1998, Rhimes made a short film, *Blossoms and Veils*, which starred Jada Pinkett-Smith and Jeffrey Wright. The film was her first and only credit as a director, and

Hank Aaron

Hank Aaron is a former American Major League Baseball (MLB) right fielder. He held the MLB record for career home runs for thirty-three years, and he still holds several other MLB records. His primary team was the Milwaukee Braves, and he is one of only two players to hit thirty or more home runs in a season at least fifteen times. In 1995, the documentary about his life, *Hank Aaron: Chasing the Dream*, was nominated for a Primetime Emmy Award. In 1996, it also received a nomination for Best Documentary at the Oscars.[3]

it led to a feature film collaboration with Pinkett-Smith and her actor and producer husband, Will Smith.[4]

Things started to look up again, and in her spare time Rhimes continued to write screenplays. One of them was a romantic comedy called *Human Seeking Same*, which was bought by the film studio New Line Cinema. Although it did not end up getting made, earning money for her script gave Rhimes a surge in confidence. It also drew the industry's attention to the budding screenwriter.

Soon enough, she was asked to write the script for *Introducing Dorothy Dandridge*, an HBO biopic starring actress Halle Berry. Berry was already a Hollywood star, having appeared in a number of movies and television shows. Playing the role of Dandridge, however, earned Berry widespread critical acclaim. She was awarded an Emmy, a

Halle Berry portayed actress, dancer, and singer Dorothy Dandridge in an acclaimed movie cowritten by Shonda Rhimes. The film tells the story of Dandridge's rise to stardom, detailing the struggles she faced as an African American performer in the 1950s.

Golden Globe, and a Screen Actors Guild award for her performance.[5]

When Rhimes addressed the graduating students at Dartmouth College, her words gave insight into the way she approached her work in the early years. During the speech, she explained that, although she had always wanted to be a writer, she did not become a writer by dreaming about it. "Dreams are lovely," she told the students, "but they are just dreams." Rhimes explained to the students that the real way for people to achieve the things they want is by doing. Even if people don't know what their passion is or what they want to do, Rhimes believes that the only way to become successful is to keep working and moving forward. This outlook would see her through the hard times to follow.

Bumps in the Road

Although Rhimes's reputation was growing in the late 1990s, the journey to success was not always a smooth one. In 1998, actors Will Smith and Jada Pinkett-Smith showed interest in producing a feature film Rhimes had written for her thesis while at USC, called *When Willows Touch*. Unfortunately, three weeks before the feature film was scheduled to begin production, one of the starring actors walked away from the project. This caused Miramax, the studio that had agreed to pay for the film, to pull the funding.

Despite the setback, Rhimes stayed focused. Hot off the success of *Introducing Dorothy Dandridge*, she was asked to write a film that would help an internationally known pop star break into the movie business. The only problem was that Rhimes didn't know who the singer was. As she told the *Hollywood Reporter*, "I remember thinking, 'Who is Britney Spears?'"[7] In order to find out, Rhimes flew to Chicago to watch the singer perform. When she arrived at the concert, she was met with thousands of screaming fans. Seeing the effect Spears had on the audience, Rhimes started to realize the potential of the project.

> "I think a lot of people dream. And while they are busy dreaming, the really happy people, the really successful people, the really interesting, powerful, engaged people, are busy doing.[6]"

Pop and Princesses

Rhimes got to work writing the script for *Crossroads*, and the movie was released in 2002. Although it wasn't well

Britney Spears

Britney Spears was born in Mississippi on December 2, 1981, and was raised in Louisiana. She acted in stage productions and television shows as a child before signing a record deal in 1997. Spears became a pop icon, and in 1999 her breakthrough single, "Baby One More Time," became an international hit. Six of her first seven albums reached number one on the *Billboard 200*, which is a record chart that ranks the 200 most popular music albums in the United States.

received by critics, it made $37 million dollars in the United States and more than $60 million worldwide. Alongside Britney Spears, it starred up-and-coming actresses Zoe Saldana (who has since starred in the *Guardians of the Galaxy* and *Avatar* franchises) and Taryn Manning (who went on to play Tiffany "Pennsatucky" Doggett in the television series *Orange Is the New Black*).

Crossroads did not receive any industry awards, but it did raise Rhimes's profile. It also provided Rhimes with enough money to buy a house in Beachwood Canyon, a community in the Hollywood Hills in California. "I called it, 'The House That Britney Bought,'" Rhimes told the *Hollywood Reporter*.

In 2001, her mentor, Debra Martin Chase, had achieved a huge success when she produced the

Britney Spears starred in *Crossroads*, a film about three friends who take a road trip across the country. Spears and her team created the idea for the film and approached Rhimes to develop and write it.

• • • • • • • • • • • • • • • • • • • •

Disney film *The Princess Diaries*. Chase was now seeking a writer for the sequel, and Rhimes was the obvious choice. Released in 2004, *The Princess Diaries 2: Royal Engagement* was not as successful at the box office as the first movie, but Rhimes treasured the experience because it gave her the opportunity

The Princess Diaries films

The Princess Diaries stars Anne Hathaway as Mia Thermopolis, a socially awkward teenager being raised by a single mom. After the death of her father, Mia finds out that she is heir to the throne in the Kingdom of Genovia, which is ruled by her grandmother, Queen Dowager Clarisse Renaldi, played by Julie Andrews.

In the sequel, *The Princess Diaries 2: Royal Engagement*, Mia turns twenty-one and is faced with a dilemma when she is given thirty days to find a husband or risk losing her chance for the throne.

to work with actress Julie Andrews. Andrews had previously appeared in the well-loved classics *Mary Poppins* (1964) and *The Sound of Music* (1965).[8]

After the movie, Rhimes wanted a change. She had fun writing for kids but decided that she wanted to write for grown-ups again. Next on her agenda was a television pilot for ABC about young war correspondents. Unfortunately, the timing of the story was not on her side. In 2003, the United States invaded Iraq, and many American troops were sent to the war zone. This made the subject of war feel too real and close to home to be entertaining. Rhimes, however, was never one to give up.

CHAPTER FIVE

"I'd Rather Have a Stubborn Girl"

• •

I n an interview with Oprah Winfrey for the *Super Soul Sunday* program, Rhimes revealed that from a young age, she always knew she would have children one day. She even thought that she would have three girls, which did indeed become her reality. Although having children was always on her mind, she was never interested in playing dress-up as a bride when she was little. From a young age, Rhimes knew that she did not want to be married.[1] Speaking to the *Hollywood Reporter* about marriage, Rhimes said, "There's pressure in our society to get married. And if you don't want it, [society asks] what's wrong with you?"[2]

Moment of Awakening

In September 2001, before her transition to television, Rhimes moved to Vermont to finish a movie script. She had just broken up with a boyfriend and decided to spend a month in a farmhouse writing. On her

September 11 Attacks

On September 11, 2001, terrorists hijacked four planes. The hijackers flew two of the planes into the twin towers of the World Trade Center in New York City. The twin towers caught fire and collapsed.

A third plane was flown into the Pentagon building, which is the headquarters of the United States' military in Arlington, Virginia. Part of the building was destroyed. The fourth plane crashed in a field in Shanksville, Pennsylvania, when the crew and passengers stopped the hijackers from reaching their target. It is believed that plane may have been heading for the White House.

Almost three thousand people were killed in the attacks, and more than six thousand people were injured. The events of September 11, 2001, are often called "9/11," referring to the ninth month and the eleventh day, which is when the attacks took place.

The hijackings were linked to the terrorist group al-Qaeda, led by Osama bin Laden. After years of hiding, he was found and killed in Pakistan on May 2, 2011, by US Navy SEALs during Barack Obama's presidency.[3]

Shonda Rhimes with her eldest daughter, named after Harper Lee, one of Rhimes's favorite authors. From a young age, Rhimes wanted to adopt children, because she knew that there were many children in the world who needed mothers.

second day there, a friend phoned her and told her to turn on the television. The date was September 11.

As Rhimes watched the 9/11 attacks unfold, she thought that now more than ever it was important to do the things she had always wanted to do.[4] She went home, hired an adoption attorney, and made plans to start her own family.[5] Nine months later, she adopted her first daughter, Harper. She is named after Harper Lee, the author of the classic 1960 novel *To Kill a Mockingbird*.

From the age of nine, Rhimes started telling people that she would like to adopt a child. She knew that there were many children in the world who needed mothers. Going through the adoption process was challenging. However, it suited Rhimes's personality. "Looking at the process of adoption, it makes sense how comfortable I was with it. I'm a former straight 'A' student. I am driven and I like goals," she wrote.[6]

> "Being a mother is not like a job, because you can't quit being a mom—you are a mother forever.[7]"

Rhimes was "euphoric" when a pregnant woman chose Rhimes to adopt her unborn child. She had a good relationship with Harper's birth mother during the pregnancy, and they spoke on the phone often. On the day Harper was born, Rhimes sat in a parking garage in Detroit four floors away from the operating room where her daughter was delivered by emergency caesarian section. Rhimes was upset that she was not invited to be in the room for the birth. Rhimes has said that she does not cry often, describing herself as having her mother's "Southern black woman stoicism" (an ability to endure difficult experiences without showing emotion), but she did cry that day in the parking garage. She cried more than she had for a very long time.

While she was in her car, Rhimes suddenly realized something—she was not able to control the situation, so the only way to deal with it was to surrender. Rhimes accepted that, although she was going to be Harper's mother, she wanted to allow the birth mother the space to give birth. She was no longer thinking about her own experience; rather, she was thinking about the birth mother's.[8] When Rhimes took Harper home, she became a single mother. In her book, she describes herself as a working mother. "I am bringing home the bacon, and frying it up in a pan," she says.[9]

And Babies Make Three

Ten years later, in 2012, Rhimes adopted her second daughter, Emerson Pearl. This time, the birth mother chose not to meet Rhimes. Although Rhimes had questions, she understood that the birth mother was taking a leap of faith and trusting that she would be a great mother. This is why, when Emerson was born, Rhimes was two states away from the birth.[11] After she brought her new daughter home, she told *Essence* magazine, "Emerson is incredibly mellow. This is a happy time—I feel so lucky."[10]

In 2013, the family welcomed a third girl, Beckett. Instead of adopting, Rhimes used a surrogate, which

Adoption & Surrogacy

Adoption is a legal process where children are transferred from their birth parent or parents to their adoptive parent or parents. After the adoption the adoptive parents become their legal parents.

Surrogacy is when another woman carries and gives birth to a baby for a couple or parent who wants to have a child. The woman carrying the baby is called the "surrogate." There are two types of surrogacy:

Artificial insemination—where the surrogate mother uses the intended father's semen to become pregnant. This means the baby will be conceived from the surrogate mother's egg.

Host surrogacy—when eggs from the intended mother, or donor eggs, are fertilized and then implanted into the surrogate mother. The surrogate mother does not use her own eggs and is not genetically related to the baby.[13]

means another woman carried her third child through pregnancy. Although she does not think it matters how a child comes into a family, she had to correct a lot of articles at the time, which reported that she had adopted again.[12]

Approach to Parenthood

Rhimes describes her parenting style as "old-school." She doesn't see her children as her friends and doesn't

The United Friends of the Children Benefit supports foster children in Los Angeles County and provides housing and education support. The charity is close to her heart as Rhimes has adopted two of her three children—her third was born via surrogacy.

treat them that way. She isn't trying to make them like her, she's trying to raise them into good citizens. One time, when her daughter Harper complained that Rhimes was going to miss a recital, Rhimes felt really bad deep down. However, she told Harper, "I work to feed and clothe you." Although it is difficult to miss some of her children's events, Rhimes does not apologize, because she knows that, as a parent, she cannot always please her children. Sometimes her work has to come first. Rhimes often compares her parenting style to her parents' style. It was the same way when they raised her—they did not apologize either, and she turned out just fine.[14]

It is very important to Rhimes that she sets an example for her daughters. She wants them to see her as a woman who works hard and has a respected job. She believes that she is a better mother because she has achieved the career she always wanted. In her book, she explains, "because I get to write all day, because I get to spend my days making things up, that woman is a better person—and a better mother. Because that woman is happy. That woman is fulfilled."[15] Sometimes, people describe being a mother as a job. Rhimes strongly disagrees with this description. She believes that being a mother is *who* she is, not *what* she is. She feels that being a mother is not like a job, because you cannot quit being a mom—you are a mother forever.[16]

Raising Girls as a Single Mother

Although she is a single mother, Rhimes does not feel like she has the same pressures that are usually

As a working single mother, one of the most important things to Rhimes is that she sets a good example for her daughters. She feels that it is important for them to see her happy and fulfilled in life.

linked to this status. She is very grateful that she is not a struggling single mom, and she tries not to use the term in a way that makes her sound like she is trying to pretend she is struggling. Rhimes is fortunate that her sisters, Delorse and Sandie, live close to her—just four blocks away. She also lives just forty minutes away from her parents.[17]

Each of Rhimes's daughters have different personalities, but they all share something in common—they are all stubborn. Although this might sound like a negative trait, Rhimes sees it as a positive. She is proud that they are all headstrong and feels that because of this, no one will ever take advantage of them. Like her, they will follow their own paths instead of being influenced by other people. In an article for *Good Housekeeping* magazine, she said having a stubborn child was so much better than having a child who can be easily manipulated. "I don't want to have a nice girl. I'd rather have a stubborn girl," she said.[18] Rhimes would like her daughters to feel like they can do anything and be anything they want to be. She does not want them to think that there are things they cannot do because they are women of color. If they grow up believing they can be anything, then she will know she has succeeded as a mother.[19]

CHAPTER SIX

Shaping ShondaLand

· · · · · · · · · · · · · · · · · ·

U p to this point, Rhimes's career had been on the rise, but in 2005 it truly took off. When it became clear that the show about war correspondents would no longer work, the ABC network asked Rhimes to come up with something else. Speaking to *Fortune* magazine in 2013, she revealed that she asked ABC, "What does Bob Iger want, what is he looking for?" Bob Iger is the CEO of the Walt Disney Company, ABC's parent company. Iger was looking for a new show for ABC. Specifically, he wanted a hospital drama, and so Rhimes set about writing *Grey's Anatomy*. Rhimes's biggest opportunity to date came about, in part, because **she** took the initiative to ask that important question.[1]

In March that year, *Grey's Anatomy* premiered on ABC, and ShondaLand productions was born. The drama focuses on the interns and staff who work in the surgical department of a Seattle, Washington, hospital. As of 2016, the show had aired for a remarkable thirteen seasons and counting.

To write the series, Rhimes drew on her past experiences working as a candy striper when she was a teenager. She also drew inspiration from watching real-life surgeries on television, describing herself as a "medical junkie." Her love for reading and research and her talent for telling stories all helped make *Grey's Anatomy* a unique and popular show.

The storylines largely focus on the medical interns who are training to become doctors. Having her own show for the first time made Rhimes feel like she could relate to the characters she was writing. She told the University of South Carolina in an interview, "You work a lot of hours, you don't get a lot of sleep, you're not entirely sure you know exactly what you're doing, but you're trying really hard to keep the 'patient' alive." The difference in Rhimes's case was that the "patient" was her television show. Even though it was hard work, Rhimes loved it. She especially liked that she could experience being a doctor without having to do all the work of becoming a doctor.[2]

Grey's Anatomy

Grey's Anatomy features an ensemble cast, meaning the regular cast members are given roughly equal amounts of screen time and equally developed storylines. Although it is set in the fictional Grey-Sloan Memorial Hospital in Seattle, the show is filmed in Los Angeles, California.

The show's name is a play on the human anatomy textbook by Henry Gray as well as the lead character's name: Meredith Grey. Although it originally was

Set in a Seattle hospital, *Grey's Anatomy* tells the story of a group of surgeon interns navigating their personal and professional lives. *Grey's Anatomy* was Rhimes's first show and is still on the air.

called *Complications*, referring to medical complications that come up in surgery, it was ultimately decided the show should be called *Grey's Anatomy*. The series follows the lives of the hospital's doctors, interns, and residents. Rhimes has multiple roles on *Grey's Anatomy*—she is the show's creator, head writer, and showrunner. She is also one of the show's executive producers, along with Betsy Beers. Executive producers bring different people's skills together to make a film or television show. They organize things like raising finances and arranging legal issues.

One of the most celebrated aspects of the show is its racial diversity. This means that the show uses a color-blind casting technique, where the ethnicity of the characters is not decided before people audition for the roles. When it first premiered, the cast had nine main cast members: Ellen Pompeo, Sandra Oh, Katherine Heigl, Justin Chambers, T.R. Knight, Chandra Wilson, James Pickens Jr., Isaiah Washington, and Patrick Dempsey. Over the years, the show has changed and expanded, and season thirteen includes just three of the original cast members: Ellen Pompeo, Chandra Wilson, and James Pickens Jr.

Highs and Lows

Although Rhimes writes drama, she never expected to be at the center of a gossip storm. In 2008, actress Katherine Heigl publicly announced that she wanted her name removed from Emmy consideration that year. She felt that writing for her character that season had not been good enough to deserve an Emmy. Although neither Rhimes nor ABC commented at the time, years later Rhimes did open up about the incident on the show *Next Chapter* with Oprah Winfrey. She said that she had felt "stung" by Heigl.[3]

Even before this incident, there had been scandal on the set of *Grey's Anatomy*. Actor Isiah Washington was fired from the show after the third season, because he had made homophobic statements to fellow cast member T.R. Knight.[4] Rhimes told Winfrey that these experiences made her a lot more careful about whom she casts on her shows. It was a very tough time in her life. Rhimes was used to being a writer, not a businesswoman and public figure. Speaking about that period of time to the *Hollywood Reporter*, she said, "I'm an introvert. That wasn't what I signed up for."[5]

> ## Spin-Off
>
> A spin-off is a radio or television program, film, or video game that derives from a show that already exists. It usually focuses on one or more characters from the original show or on an aspect of the original show, such as a location, event, or topic. In the case of *Private Practice*, one of the characters, Dr. Montgomery, left the Seattle hospital in *Grey's Anatomy* and moved to the Los Angeles hospital in *Private Practice*.

Despite the bumps in the road, *Grey's Anatomy* is one of the highest-rated dramas among people aged eighteen to forty-nine in the United States. At one point, it was one of the top-ten-rated shows in the United States. It is also the longest-running scripted primetime show currently airing on ABC and is the second-longest scripted primetime show ever to air on ABC. The show has won numerous awards and is a commercial success. In 2012, it earned the fifth-highest advertising revenue.[6]

Not-So-*Private Practice*

Following the success of *Grey's Anatomy*, Rhimes created a spin-off series in 2007, *Private Practice*. Also set in a hospital, the show followed Dr. Addison Montgomery (played by Kate Walsh) as she left Seattle

Grace Hospital for a hospital in Los Angeles. The main series cast included Tim Daly, Amy Brenneman, Audra McDonald, and Taye Diggs. Due to a writer's strike, the first season of *Private Practice* had to be shortened to nine episodes.[7] The strike was known as the Television Writers' Strike, and twelve thousand screen and television writers took part to demand better pay. It started on November 5, 2007, and ended on February 12, 2008.[8] *Private Practice* was set up during a season three episode of *Grey's Anatomy* and ran for six seasons. The series finale was aired January 22, 2013.

By this point, Rhimes had truly hit the big time. Although she was confident in her work as a writer and showrunner, she wasn't used to the fame that came along with it. Being an introvert and a writer, she found the attention difficult. She told Oprah Winfrey in an interview, "At that moment in time, I was really terrified by what was happening, because I was a writer who stayed home in her pajamas and suddenly people in the grocery store were shouting lines of dialogue at me."[9]

> "At that moment in time, I was really terrified by what was happening, because I was a writer who stayed home in her pajamas and suddenly people in the grocery store were shouting lines of dialogue at me."

Scandalous Success

In 2011, Rhimes was the executive producer for a new ABC medical drama, *Off the Map*, created by *Grey's Anatomy* writer Jenna Bans. It focused on a group of doctors who practiced medicine at a remote clinic in the Amazon. The ABC network officially canceled the series in May 2011.

That same month, ABC agreed to take on a new television series written by Rhimes. *Scandal* is a political thriller focusing on the work of fictional crisis manager Olivia Pope. The character is inspired by Judy Smith, aide to President George H.W. Bush. The show made its debut in April 2012 and stars Kerry Washington, who became the first African American lead actress in a network series in thirty-seven years.[10]

Who Is Judy Smith?

Judy Smith is a United States crisis manager, lawyer, author, and television producer. She was born October 27, 1958, and is the founder, president, and CEO of the crisis management firm Smith & Company. In March 1991 Smith worked alongside President George H.W. Bush as his special assistant and deputy press secretary. It is her work in crisis management that caught the eye of producer Betsy Beers, and it became the inspiration behind the television series *Scandal*.[12]

Shonda Rhimes and the cast of *Scandal* accepted the NAACP Image Award for Outstanding Drama Series. Set in Washington, DC, the show focuses on a crisis management firm and staff at the White House, and it was Rhimes's third phenomenal hit.

By this time, Rhimes was starting to find the business side of the television industry easier. Although the early days were tough and sometimes made her want to hide away, over time she really started to enjoy it all and began to have fun.[11] Little did she know that just around the corner, another big change was on the horizon.

A year later, on November 28, 2013, Rhimes was with her sister Delorse. Delorse was preparing Thanksgiving dinner, and Shonda was in the kitchen helping. Rhimes told Delorse about some of the glamorous entertainment industry events to which she had been invited. She sometimes felt like her family was not impressed by the success she had achieved, so she often talked about these great events as a way to impress them. This rarely worked. In her book, Rhimes explains that her family loves her a lot, but they don't give her special treatment because she is a celebrity. They have known her since she was the little girl in thick glasses, who once threw up alphabet soup all over the back porch. This has helped Rhimes to stay grounded over the years.

While she was telling Delorse about all of the invitations she had received, Delorse did not seem interested. This made Rhimes talk about it more and more, until finally, Delorse interrupted her and asked, "Are you going to do any of these things?" This caught Rhimes by surprise. The truth was, she was not planning to go to any of the events. She very rarely did; she always told herself she was too busy, but really she was afraid. That day, Delorse pointed out that Rhimes never said "yes" to anything, and she realized just how much life she was missing out on. On that day, Rhimes made a promise to herself; she was going to start saying "yes" to everything for a whole year. She found, however, that saying "yes" was not always as simple as it sounded.[13]

Being Good at What You Do

Next on Rhimes's television show list was *How to Get Away with Murder*. ABC announced in December 2013 that it would be made by ShondaLand productions. The show was officially picked up in 2014. It stars Viola Davis as the lead character. Although it is produced by ShondaLand, Rhimes did not actually create or write the show. Peter Nowalk, who had worked as a writer on *Grey's Anatomy* and then as a producer on *Scandal*, created and wrote it.[14]

Shonda Rhimes with actress Viola Davis, star of *How to Get Away with Murder*. The series was created by Peter Nowalk, a former writer on *Scandal* and executive producer on *Grey's Anatomy*. Although it is produced by Rhimes, she does not write the show.

In 2015, ShondaLand took on a new television project, *The Catch*, based on a novel by Kate Atkinson. The show is a mystery-thriller about a private investigator who is about to get married, but her husband-to-be is conning her. It stars Mireille Enos and Peter Krause and was created by Jennifer Schuur, Kate Atkinson, and Helen Gregor. As opposed to writing the show, Rhimes works alongside Betsy Beers as an executive producer. *The Catch* premiered on ABC in March 2016, taking over *How to Get Away with Murder*'s time slot after the end of *Murder*'s second season.[15]

With so many projects in production, Rhimes is constantly writing and working. In 2013, she told *Vanity Fair* about an unusual source for many of her story ideas—overheard conversations. She listens to people talking and takes notes on her iPhone. Rhimes has several other writing techniques that she could not live without. For example, once she has written a script, Rhimes will always read it aloud. This is a useful way to check that the dialogue sounds right. She also swears by getaways and breaks where she can write completely uninterrupted. To balance this, she now makes sure she has weekends where she does not do any work at all. This is a rule she had to make when Harper, her eldest daughter, was five years old. Rhimes found that she was exhausted from working too much all the time, and she made the rule to have work-free weekends when she could spend quality time with her family. "There is no work that is so urgent that on

Monday morning I couldn't pick it back up," she told the *LA Times*.[16]

In 2014, Rhimes signed a deal with ABC Studios, which will keep her at the network until at least 2018. The once introverted child, who had goofy glasses and loved to read, is now referred to as "the first lady of television drama."[17] She has become one of the most powerful writers and producers in television and is also currently the most powerful African American

ShondaLand Productions

ShondaLand is the television production company founded by Shonda Rhimes in 2005. The company has since gone on to produce all of her other shows.

Grey's Anatomy: March 27, 2005–present

Private Practice: September 26, 2007–January 22, 2013

Off the Map: January 12, 2011–April 6, 2011

Scandal: April 5, 2012–present

How to Get Away with Murder: September 25, 2014–present

The Catch: September 25, 2014–present

Still Star-Crossed: In development, due 2017

female showrunner in television. When questioned about her success, Rhimes says it is her competitive nature that has helped get her where she is today. Being competitive always made her want to be the best that she could be. As she puts it, "I like to be really good at what I'm doing. It's important."[18]

Many, many years after Rhimes had dreams of becoming the next Toni Morrison, she ended up having dinner with her idol. In a strange twist of fate, all Morrison wanted to talk about was *Grey's Anatomy*. This was the moment where Rhimes fully realized the scope of her achievements. Choosing her own path had made her successful. Rhimes would never have achieved any of it if she had continued to dream about being her idol, instead of focusing on becoming herself.[19]

CHAPTER SEVEN

First. Only. Different.

• •

R himes was building successful television show upon successful television show. Thursday nights on ABC were ShondaLand nights. From *Grey's Anatomy* to *Private Practice*, then *Scandal* to *How to Get Away with Murder*—Rhimes was both entertaining the nation and bringing in the ratings. In the world of network television, it is unusual for shows to run longer than three seasons. Most of Rhimes's shows have run at least five.

Along with the success, however, came pressure. "The network expected me to maintain the quality of the [shows] currently on air...I started having nightmares about getting cancelled," she wrote.[1] Rhimes's sister Delorse worried about her. She became concerned that the stress would affect Rhimes's creativity. On the contrary, the cause of Rhimes's nightmares was not the writing or all the work that went into making the shows. She loved creating characters and worlds for them to exist in. ShondaLand felt just like the days

when she made up stories in her mother's pantry—it was just bigger. Making up stories was, and always will be, where Rhimes feels most at ease. Her worry was not about writing or making the shows, but about the rising expectations. The more successful the shows were, the more pressure there was not to fail. And failure was not an option, because of who she is—an African American woman.[2]

F.O.D.

As Rhimes's career progressed, the stakes became higher. By just being herself, she had managed to create shows that were different. When Rhimes made her first show, she wrote it in a way that reflected twenty-first-century society. The world of the show included people of all races, genders, backgrounds, and sexual orientations. This felt normal to her—she just made her characters look

As Rhimes's career progressed and her success rose, so did the pressure to perform. Given that she was the first African American woman to have several shows back-to-back in a primetime slot on a television channel, she was determined to keep making hits.

and feel like real people. "People of color live three-dimensional lives, have love stories and are not funny sidekicks, cliches or criminals," she explains in her book.[3] She created a world where women could be both heroes and villains, and where people of color could be bosses. To Rhimes this was all obvious, but in the world of television, it had not been done before. Rhimes is seen as brave and trailblazing.

Rhimes was breaking the mold and proving the industry wrong—people were interested in watching shows that starred people from all backgrounds and races. This increased the pressure she felt. As her career advanced, Rhimes started to notice that she was the *first* African American woman to do what she was doing. She was also the *only* African American woman to do what she was doing. It was not just her work that was breaking the mold, but she was too. She was *different*. Rhimes became what she refers to as a "First. Only. Different.", or F.O.D. As she explains, "Second chances are for future generations. That is what you're building when you're an F.O.D."

To Rhimes, being an F.O.D. means there is no room to make mistakes. *Scandal* was the first network drama in thirty-seven years to feature a female African American main character. If it did not get high enough ratings, then networks would be less likely to make other shows starring an African American actress. "Failure mean[s] two generations of actresses might have to wait for another chance to be seen as more than a sidekick," she writes.[4] Rhimes really wants everything to be perfect, because if it is not, she would feel like it is all her fault. She works so hard because she does not want to be responsible for that failure. "I [don't] want to feel like somebody [will] say, 'We had a show with an African-American lead but it failed,' and have it be my fault," she explained, in a radio interview on *Fresh Air* with Terry Gross.[5]

Building an Empire

Rhimes's first job as a showrunner helped her write the new intern characters on *Grey's Anatomy*. She felt she could relate to their experiences of being at the beginning of their careers. She later began to relate to the experiences of *Scandal's* main character, Olivia Pope. After all, Pope was also an F.O.D., the only difference was that she worked in politics instead of television. Both politics and the television industry are male dominated, so Rhimes had firsthand experience to help when writing Pope's character.

> "I think I'm most proud of the fact that I have figured out how to exist as both a creative person and artist, and a businesswoman and manager. Because those two things do not go together.[6]"

In an episode of *Scandal*, Olivia Pope has a conversation with her father. He tells her that as an African American woman, she will have to be twice as good to get half as much in life. That conversation

Sandra Oh and Shonda Rhimes celebrated the *Grey's Anatomy* Golden Globe award for Best Television Series—Drama. Oh played the role of Dr. Cristina Yang for ten seasons of the show and won the Best Supporting Actress award at the 2006 Golden Globes.

was something that had always been at the back of Rhimes's mind from the beginning and was a belief she took very seriously. But being Shonda Rhimes, she did not want *half*. She wanted it *all*. As a result, she set out to work four times as hard. She knew that whether she liked it or not, she was a role model. Not only to her own daughters, but to all women, especially women of color, and this helped drive her to succeed.[7]

Her determination and work ethic can often be seen in the characters she writes. In an interview with ABC's *Nightline*, she explained how she put herself into *Grey's Anatomy* character Dr. Cristina Yang: "The two of us had so many similarities. We [are] very intense about our work...our work ethic and our feelings about relationships are very similar."[8]

Lonely at the Top

Working hard had its benefits, but also some huge drawbacks. By putting so much energy into her work, Rhimes was exhausted outside of work. She found herself too tired to have difficult conversations in her personal life, and this meant she would find herself in situations where she felt taken advantage of and unhappy. This made her want to spend more time in the office, because at work she was the boss and was in control. However, her private life really started to suffer.

Rhimes had declined invitations to social events so many times that she stopped being invited to things. She would get angry emails from friends for missing birthdays, and some of her social circle thought that she'd abandoned them for a glamorous life in Hollywood. This could not have been further from

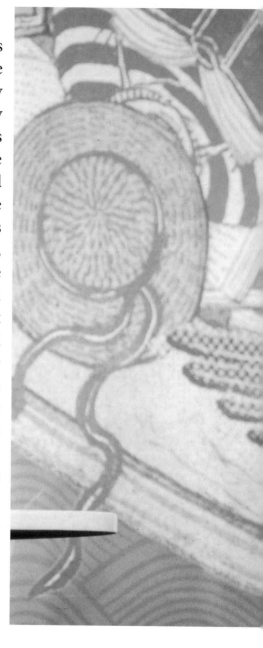

68

Having spent a lot of time alone as an introverted child, Rhimes understands what it feels like to be isolated. She often writes about loneliness in her shows and has discussed in interviews how, through becoming a writer, she eventually found her "tribe."

the truth: Rhimes spent all of her time either working or staying home, often alone.

During this period of her life, Rhimes felt like she was losing herself. Slowly but surely, as she turned down invitation after invitation, she became quite lonely. Being an F.O.D., there was no other person in her exact same situation, so she had few people that she could confide in and who would understand her. And so she threw herself even further into her work.

Reasons to Get Healthy

The more Rhimes worked, the more exhausted she became. The more exhausted she became, the more stressed she was. And the more stressed she was, the more she ate. At first, she did not think too much of her weight. As a feminist, Rhimes believes that women should be able to look however they want. She did not like to question her own weight, because she did not want to judge herself. She wanted to be free to look however she chose, and she thought that worrying about how she looked might be shallow. She strongly believes that looks do not matter; only her brain matters. Her body was just a container to carry her brain.[9]

This outlook was working fine, until gradually, Rhimes started to feel unhealthy. Her clothes got tighter as she went up higher and higher in dress size. Eventually, she needed the largest size available in a plus-size clothing store. This, coupled with not being able to buckle her seat belt on an airplane, made Rhimes pause and think about her body and her weight. She was right about her body being a container to carry her brain, "but so is a car," she writes in her book. "And if the car is broken down and busted, my brain isn't going anywhere." She realized that her body would only be capable of carrying her brain if it was healthy, and she did not feel healthy.[10]

People around her tried to help, but it was very difficult at first. Her colleague Betsy Beers told Rhimes to train herself to love salads. After this, Rhimes didn't speak to her for three days. "What kind of sicko trains themselves to love salads?!" she thought to herself. On another occasion, her personal trainer told her that "nothing tastes as good as thin feels." Rhimes did not like his condescending tone, so she fired him.[11] In time though, Rhimes realized that she was overeating to make herself feel better. When things got tough in her life, she found that overeating helped her deal with it. Although it did feel good at the time, it was not good for either her emotional well-being or her weight. She started to face her feelings rather than suppress them with food. In the past, she avoided confronting people who had upset her and instead turned to food to make herself feel better. On March 8, 2014, a little while after Rhimes started her quest to say "yes" more, putting food on top of her feelings no longer felt like an option. She decided it was time to say "yes" to being healthy. The determination to become healthier came from the same place that helped Rhimes achieve her career—her desire to succeed in everything she does. By March 1, 2015, Rhimes had lost one hundred pounds.[12]

And the Award Goes To...

As Rhimes was the first African American woman to create and executive produce a top ten network series, it is no surprise that her achievements have been celebrated by many well-known awards organizations in entertainment. In 2005, the year that *Grey's Anatomy* first aired, Rhimes was awarded the *Chicago Tribune* newspaper's Chicagoan of the Year in the Arts. The accolade celebrates "talented artists and cultural tastemakers."[13]

In 2007, Rhimes won a Golden Globe Award for Best Television Series—Drama for *Grey's Anatomy*. In her acceptance speech, she thanked the whole cast, sharing that "every last one of them makes an outstanding contribution to the show."[14] That same year, she won *Glamour* magazine's Woman of the Year award, which chooses women from all over the world who are excelling in their field.[15]

List of Shonda Rhimes's Notable Awards and Nominations

2006, Emmy—Outstanding Writing for a Drama Series: Nominee

2006, Emmy—Outstanding Drama Series: Nominee

2006, Writers Guild of America—New Series: Winner

2007, Emmy—Outstanding Drama Series: Nominee

2007, Golden Globe—Best Drama Series: Winner

2007, PGA Award—Outstanding Producer of Episodic Television, Drama: Winner

2007, NAACP Image Award—Outstanding Writing in a Dramatic Series: Winner

2008, PGA Award—Outstanding Producer of Episodic Television, Drama: Nominee

2009, NAACP Image Award—Outstanding Writing in a Dramatic Series: Winner

2010, NAACP Image Award—Outstanding Writing in a Dramatic Series: Winner

2011, NAACP Image Award—Outstanding Writing in a Dramatic Series: Winner

2012, GLAAD—Golden Gate Award: Winner

2013, TV Guide Awards—Fan Favorite Awards: Winner

2013, Women's Image Network Awards—Outstanding Film/Show Written by a Woman: Winner

2014, Directors Guild of America Awards—Diversity Award: Winner

2015, Writers Guild Award—Paddy Chayefsky Laurel Award for Television Writing Achievement: Winner

2016, Producers Guild Award—Norman Lear Achievement Award in Television: Winner

2016, International Emmy—Founders Award: Winner

Although Rhimes believes passionately in diversity, she is also careful to present it organically. Her shows are often praised for including LGBTQ storylines and actors of different ethnicities. Rhimes simply sees it as reflecting normal life.

Every year from 2007 to 2011, Rhimes won NAACP Image Awards for either *Grey's Anatomy* or *Private Practice*. The awards are presented by the American National Association for the Advancement of Colored People to honor outstanding people of color in film, television, music, and literature. From 2013 to 2016, she received nominations for *Scandal* and *Grey's Anatomy* and was named Entertainer of the Year.

In 2009, Rhimes received the Mary Pickford Foundation Award from the University of Southern California's School of Cinematic Arts, which is where she did her postgraduate study. Each year, the award is given to a former USC student "whose extraordinary achievements bring special distinction to the USC School of Cinematic Arts and to the industry."[16]

In 2012, Rhimes won the GLAAD Golden Gate Award. The GLAAD Media Awards recognize and honor the media for their inclusive representations of the lesbian, gay, bisexual, and transgender (LGBT) community and the issues that affect their lives. After the controversy surrounding Isaiah Washington's homophobic comments, it was an honor for Rhimes's efforts in including gay characters to be recognized. "I think that love is universal," she said in her acceptance speech. "In telling LGBT stories, I'm telling everyone's story."[17]

Rhimes has also been twice included in *TIME* magazine's 100 Most Influential People list, as well as *Fortune* magazine's 50 Most Powerful Women in Business. She was appointed by President Obama to serve as a trustee for the John F. Kennedy Center for the Performing Arts in 2013 and won the Writers Guild Paddy Chayefsky Laurel Award in 2015. [18]

After receiving several Emmy nominations for *Grey's Anatomy*, in 2016 it was announced that Rhimes would receive the honorary International Emmy Founders Award. The award was presented to her by her colleague, Tony Goldwyn, who plays President Fitzgerald Grant on *Scandal*.[19] Earlier in the year, Rhimes had been awarded the Norman Lear Award from the Producers Guild of America (PGA). On accepting the award, Rhimes said, "The fact that the award is named after a legendary producer whose work has had such an inspiring effect on my growth as a writer is genuinely gratifying. I couldn't be more grateful for this special recognition."[20]

CHAPTER EIGHT

"You Are Not Alone"

· ·

One of the things that makes Shonda Rhimes stand out in both her career and personal life is her sense of identity. Rhimes has strong values and beliefs that have steered her through life and influenced the decisions she has made. At the Human Rights Campaign Gala in 2015, Rhimes took to the stage and announced, "I'm standing here to tell you: you are not alone. Your tribe of people, they are out there in the world. Waiting for you."[1]

Throughout the duration of her speech, Rhimes talked about how being lonely when she was younger drove her to write. As she didn't really have friends and people were sometimes quite mean to her, she felt very alone growing up. This loneliness made her want to write characters and stories that felt like they were her friends. She told the crowd at the gala that this was the beginning of ShondaLand, and that it had existed since she was eleven years old. Making up

Rhimes had thick glasses as a teenager and felt socially awkward. She rarely spoke and didn't have lots of friends. Rather than being around people, she felt more comfortable either reading or making up stories.

stories was somewhere that she could find company until she found friends in the real world.

Although Rhimes has written hundreds of hours of television, there is a theme that all of her stories share. That theme is loneliness. Through all her stories, she explores the idea of being alone—the fear of being alone, looking for other people so that we aren't alone, the joy of finding people who make us feel less alone, and the sadness of being left alone. All the stories she writes are in some way connected to the idea of loneliness and trying to cure it.[3]

Driving Diversity

Rhimes is often praised for her diverse casting choices; her characters are rarely written with a specific race in mind. Although she knows that this is a good thing, because it means that people from all races and walks of life get included in her shows, she does not see it as something that makes her a pioneer. Speaking to the *New York Times* in 2013, she said, "I think it's sad, and weird, and strange that it's still a thing. Somebody else needs to get their act together. And, oh, by the way, it works. Ratings-wise, it works."[4]

Including a diverse cast isn't the only thing Rhimes did differently, but it was also how she included

> "I don't know if anyone has noticed but I only ever write about one thing: being alone. The fear of being alone, the desire to not be alone...The need to hear the words: You are not alone.[2]"

79

Rhimes joined her *Scandal* stars Kerry Washington and Portia de Rossi and de Rossi's wife, Ellen DeGeneres, at the GLAAD Media Awards. Rhimes has been praised for featuring LGBTQ characters.

them. Even though there are characters of many different ethnicities, their race doesn't usually come up as a topic. Rhimes did this for a reason, as she explains: "When people who aren't of color create a show and they have one character of color on their show, that character spends all their time talking about the world as 'I'm a black man blah, blah, blah.'" Rhimes, however, doesn't believe that is how the world really works. Although she is a black woman and proud of it, it is not the only thing she talks about—her thoughts and feelings are wide and varied. Yes, she is a woman of color, but it is not the only thing that defines her.[5]

Even though Rhimes has done a lot to add to diversity in television, she does not spend a lot of time obsessing about it. She believes that, for a society to be truly equal for everyone, we should try to stop measuring things by race and gender. She simply hires the best actor or actress for the roles being cast.[6] She has said publicly that she does not like the word "diversity," because it suggests something rare or unusual. Rhimes doesn't think it is unusual at all to tell stories about women, people of color, and members of the LGBTQ+ community.

Rather than call it "diversity," Rhimes prefers to see it as "normalizing." "I'm normalizing TV. I am making TV look like the world looks," she told the audience at the Human Rights Campaign Gala.[7] In 2012, when she won the GLAAD Award, she told the

LGBTQ+

LGBTQ+ is an acronym that stands for lesbian, gay, bisexual, transgender, queer, and more. It is used to designate a community of people whose sexual or gender identities can create shared political and social concerns.

Lesbian: A woman who is attracted to other women.

Gay: A man who is attracted to other men.

Bisexual: An individual who is attracted to both genders.

Transgender: Individuals whose gender identities do not match their biological sex. For example, somebody who is assigned female at birth and identifies as a man.

Queer: Those who do not identify as either gender, or who do not identify as one specific sexuality or gender.

audience that she writes the stories she does because "love should be universal." GLAAD was founded in 1985 in response to a New York newspaper's reporting

> "I'm a black woman every day, and I'm not confused about that. I'm not worried about that.[9]"

of HIV and AIDS. One thousand people protested outside of the newspaper's offices. The organization, which stands for the Gay and Lesbian Alliance Against Defamation, held its first GLAAD Media Awards in 1990. GLAAD works with news sources to bring people stories from the LGBTQ+ community. It also steps in to respond when the LGBTQ+ community is represented unfairly.[8]

The Civil Rights Movement

The civil rights movement of the 1950s and 1960s led to the Civil Rights Act of 1964. The movement was led in part by Martin Luther King Jr., who started nonviolent protests to achieve equal rights for all, regardless of skin color, gender, nationality, religion, disability, or age. The aim of the movement, which reached its peak in the 1960s, was to ensure that the rights of all people are equal and are protected by the law. Civil rights also include the right to free speech and the right to a fair trial.

Rhimes has had many heartwarming experiences with viewers of her shows. She frequently gets approached by people who tell her how much her stories have helped them, either in "coming out" as gay to their friends and family, or from parents who were able to better understand their LGBTQ+ children because of her shows.

Rhimes believes it is important to tell LGBTQ+ stories not just for members of that community, but also to educate people outside the community. She feels that if people are not shown stories about different kinds of love, then they will be less accepting of people's differences. One day, Rhimes was asked why

she had many gay characters in her television shows. Her response was that she believed everyone should get to see themselves reflected on television, and

Martin Luther King Jr. led the civil rights movement during the 1950s and 1960s to advocate for equality for people of color. Rhimes believes she is fighting for the rights of the LGBTQ community to see themselves reflected in popular media.

that she loves all of her gay and lesbian friends. She compares this to the civil rights movement, which her grandmother and her parents experienced.[10] The civil rights movement also fought against intolerance of people's differences.

Everyone Has a Tribe

Although a lot of focus is put on the women, people of color, and LGBTQ+ characters within ShondaLand, Rhimes's aim is to represent everyone in her stories. She wants anyone, from any background, to be able to tune into her shows and see a character that they can relate to. Equally, she wants people to get to see characters who aren't like them. She strongly believes that when we are exposed to different things, we become more accepting. In *Year of Yes*, Rhimes appeals directly to her young readers with reassurance. "If you are a kid and you are out there and you are chubby and not so cute and nerdy and shy and invisible and in pain, whatever your race, whatever your gender, whatever your sexual orientation, I'm standing here to tell you: you are not alone. Your tribe of people, they are out there in the world. Waiting for you."[11]

Being confident in your abilities, being proud of who you are, and accepting yourself, are all traits that have helped Rhimes along the way—especially after deciding to say "yes" more. In doing that, she found a new level of confidence. She believes that a negative attitude makes it difficult to see any positive in situations. Before the *Year of Yes*, she was turning down invitations, hiding away, overeating, and

Sometimes the pressures and demands of the job made Rhimes retreat into herself and her work. At times, she felt quite lonely. It was difficult to find anyone who understood her exact situation and the challenges she faced as an F.O.D.

overworking. Although her career was a success, it didn't all come together until she really started to embrace life and get involved with things again.

Rhimes knows what it feels like to lack confidence, and so she has advice for others in similar situations. She advises people to do voluntary work, in order to focus on something outside of one's self. "Devote a slice of your energies toward making the world suck less every week...whether you are a legacy or the first in your family to go to college, the air you are breathing right now is rare air. Appreciate it."[12]

CHAPTER NINE

"Don't Call Me Lucky"

• • • • • • • • • • • • • • • •

Shonda Rhimes's journey to the present has been one of hard work and steep learning. Although she was always a natural writer, she wasn't born a showrunner and leader; these are things she had to learn. Ever since the first episode of *Grey's Anatomy* in 2005, she has had to learn how to mold herself from the excited writer who was given the opportunity to write television shows, into a boss.[1] That's not to say she does not still enjoy the writing side. In fact, the writing is what keeps her going. "As long as I'm writing things that make me happy and I'm enjoying [myself], it doesn't feel like work," she told the University of Southern California during an interview. It has always been her goal to make her work not feel like work.[2]

With *Grey's Anatomy* in its thirteenth season, *Scandal* in its sixth, *How to Get Away with Murder* in its third, and *The Catch* in its second, ShondaLand is in full swing. The newest addition, *Still Star-Crossed*, is a period drama based on a book by Melinda Taub. The book is a sequel of sorts to William Shakespeare's play *Romeo and Juliet*. *Romeo and Juliet* is about a young couple who want to be together but can't, because their families are at war with each other. It ends with the tragic deaths of the two main characters. *Still Star-Crossed* takes place after the deaths of *Romeo and Juliet*, when a prince tries to end the feud between the two families by forcing Rosaline, Juliet's cousin, and Benvolio, Romeo's cousin, to get married against their will.

Old Tale, New Faces

Still Star-Crossed is a period drama, which means it is a drama set in a historic time period. It is an unusual choice for ShondaLand, as every other

Rhimes is able to balance work and pleasure, and occasionally she gets to combine the two. Here, she attends the Palais des Festivals in beautiful Cannes, France, with colleagues Tony Goldwyn, Betsy Beers, and Mireille Enos.

show has been set in the present, which has helped allow the diverse casting. Period dramas very rarely feature cast members of different races, and usually the characters are mostly Caucasian. As a ShondaLand show, Rhimes saw this as an opportunity to break the casting mold for period dramas, and two of the three main characters are actors of color.

Grey's Anatomy and *Scandal* writer Heather Mitchell created and developed the show, which was ordered on May 12, 2016. The show stars Lashana Lynch as Rosaline and Wade Briggs as Benvolio. Shonda Rhimes and Betsy Beers are executive producers on the series, along with ABC Studios and the MrG Production Company.

Doing It All

Even with everything Rhimes has achieved, she still needs to remind herself of her success. Every morning in the shower, she recites her favorite Muhammad Ali quote: "It's not bragging if you can back it up."[3] Ali was an American boxer and activist. He was originally known as Cassius Clay, but he converted to Islam and changed his name to Muhammad Ali. During his career, Ali won many boxing championships, and he is viewed as an African American icon.

Rhimes often gets asked, "How do you do it all?" To the outside world, it really does seem like she has it all: a family, a string of hit shows, and one of the highest-ranking jobs in network television. In her book, Rhimes answers this question. How does Rhimes do it all? She doesn't. Or at least, she does not feel like she does it all. She feels that, if she is doing very well in one part of her life, then she is probably not doing so well in another. If she is putting extra time and effort into making her daughters' Halloween costumes, then she is probably not paying as much attention to a script she needs to write. And if she is working hard on a script or show, then she is probably missing bath time with her daughters at home. She describes this as the "trade-off"—where one thing has to be traded for another. She says that if she is succeeding at one thing, then she is failing at another.[4] All in all, it is about finding a balance and making sure she spends some time with everything. It might mean she misses the filming of a scene or that she misses one of her daughter's swimming lessons, but overall nothing is neglected.

> "I am not lucky. You know what I am? I am smart, I am talented, I take advantage of the opportunities that come my way and I work really, really hard.[5]"

Shonda at Home

Although life for Rhimes is a juggling act between work and family, she enjoys pursuing her own hobbies when she has the time. In her house, she has a secret closet containing all sorts of materials for making crafts, from jewelry to quilts and every crafting pursuit in between.

She is also a fan of binge watching television shows. She watched every episode of *Fringe* within three weeks, followed by all of *Game of Thrones* and *The Wire*.

A more recent obsession, since deciding to become healthier during her "Year of Yes," is the rush of endorphins she gets from exercise. As a result, she exercises on her treadmill for one hour a day, while watching television. Her favorite nonscripted television show is the *National Spelling Bee*, an annual spelling bee held in Washington, DC, which she also live blogs under a pseudonym.[6]

Just like when she was younger, Rhimes is still an avid reader. Rhimes loves Harper Lee's novel *To Kill a Mockingbird*, and she has read the book over and over again since she was eleven years old. She feels that the experience of reading this books changes as she grows older. As a child, she focused her attention on the young girl character, Scout. As an adult, she finds herself investing more in the storylines of the father, Atticus, and the reclusive neighbor, Boo Radley. "It's timeless and perfect; I can't wait to share a copy with my daughters," she wrote for *Redbook* magazine. "Especially with my daughter named Harper." She also reads *Little Women*, by Louisa May Alcott, every time she goes through a relationship breakup.[7]

Getting Political

Rhimes is a vocal supporter of the Democratic Party, and she supported Hillary Clinton's bid for president of the United States. In March, 2016 Rhimes appeared alongside several stars from her ShondaLand shows (Ellen Pompeo of *Grey's Anatomy*, Kerry Washington of *Scandal*, and Viola Davies from *How to Get Away with Murder*) in a commercial for Hillary Clinton's campaign.[8]

Despite her personal politics, Rhimes did not purposely set out to include her political beliefs in the ShondaLand shows. In an interview with ABC News, she revealed that by coincidence, some of the storylines made up in her shows started to reflect real life. Even though she was not intentionally trying to reflect current political issues, some elements that had already been filmed started to look like events occurring in the real world. "It got a little scary because we had all kinds of crazy things planned and I keep walking in the room going 'Well, we can't do that, because it's real, and people will think we're stealing from actual life.' Life has surpassed anything that we could come up with." Although she has her own political opinions, Rhimes believes that it does not matter what side a person is on—Democrat or Republican. What really matters is taking an interest in politics and being engaged and politically active. "If you believe in something you should be canvassing, you should be registering people to vote, you should be doing something," she told ABC News.[9]

The International Emmy Awards took place two weeks after the results of the 2016 presidential election, in which the Republican candidate Donald Trump became the president-elect. During Rhimes's acceptance speech, she said that many people,

Rhimes believes that it is important to be engaged in politics, regardless of which party a person supports. In 2016, she took the stage at a Get Out the Vote concert in support of Hillary Clinton's presidential campaign.

including people of color, immigrants, Muslims, people with disabilities, women, and the LGBTQ+ community, were nervous about what the election result means for them. This is because the president-elect has not always demonstrated a support for minority groups.

During the acceptance speech, Rhimes had a moment when her thinking shifted. Previously, when asked about the diversity in her writing and casting, Rhimes always explained that she was merely reflecting the world around us. She now realized that the shows she created could be even more meaningful and powerful. As people around her became increasingly more afraid that their voices were not being heard, Rhimes vowed that she would continue to speak for them and make their voices heard through her shows. "I've had the luxury of living in a free and fair America where I slept peacefully under the ideals of equality and the making of a more perfect union. The ideals are still there; whether or not we're actually going to live up to them is the question," she told the audience.[10] Rhimes will continue to write these characters in the same way she has always done, but after the election results, she will be doing so with more purpose.

Rhimes and her ShondaLand actors attended the White House Correspondents Dinner in 2016. The event is a chance for Hollywood and Washington to collide.

Fairy Tale Endings

Among all of Rhimes's achievements, she revealed to Oprah Winfrey that she is most proud of "the fact that I have figured out how to exist as both a creative person and artist, and a businesswoman and manager. Because

Shonda Rhimes Filmography

1995: *Hank Aaron: Chasing the Dream*

1998: *Blossoms and Veils*

1999: *Introducing Dorothy Dandridge*

2002: *Crossroads*

2004: *The Princess Diaries 2: Royal Engagement*

2005–present: *Grey's Anatomy*

2007–2013: *Private Practice*

2009: *Inside the Box*

2009: *Seattle Grace: On Call*

2009: *Seattle Grace: Message of Hope*

2011: *Off the Map*

2012: *Gilded Lilys*

2012–present: *Scandal*

2014–present: *How to Get Away with Murder*

2016–present: *The Catch*

Expected 2017: *Still Star-Crossed*

Rhimes has achieved the ultimate goal for a writer: she has written her own fairy tale. Her imagination and, most important, hard work have allowed her to succeed as both a creative artist and a businesswoman.

those two things do not go together."[11] Although Rhimes was never one to dream of wearing a beautiful wedding gown and marrying her prince, she has very much achieved her own fairy tale.

In her world, women get to choose what they want their fairy tale ending to be. In her world, girls don't have to settle for the fairy tale they've been told they are supposed to have. In her world, with self-belief, hard work, and passion, everyone's fairy tale ending is within reach.[12]

One thing Rhimes doesn't believe in, however, is dreaming toward that fairy tale. Addressing graduating students during her Dartmouth commencement speech, she imparted, "It's hard work that makes things happen. It's hard work that creates change. Ditch the dream and be a doer, not a dreamer."[13]

Chronology

1970 Shonda Lynn Rhimes is born on January 13, 1970, in University Park, Chicago.

1987 Graduates from Marian Catholic High School.

1991 Graduates from Dartmouth College.

1994 Graduates with an MFA from the University of Southern California School of Cinema and Television; awarded the Gary Rosenberg Writing Fellowship.

1995 *Hank Aaron: Chasing the Dream* is released.

1998 Writes and directs the short film *Blossoms and Veils*.

2002 Adopts daughter Harper; *Crossroads* is released.

2004 *The Princess Diaries 2* is released.

2005 *Grey's Anatomy* first airs; ShondaLand is created.

2006 Awarded Best New Series accolade for *Grey's Anatomy* by the Writers Guild of America.

2007 *Private Practice* airs; *Grey's Anatomy* wins Best Drama at the Golden Globes.

2009–2011 Awarded the NAACP Image Award for Outstanding Writing in a Dramatic Series.

2012 Adopts daughter Emerson Pearl; *Scandal* airs and receives GLAAD Golden Gate Award.

2013 Daughter Beckett is born via surrogate; *Private Practice* ends.

2014 *How to Get Away with Murder* airs; delivers Dartmouth commencement speech.

2015 Wins Writers Guild Paddy Chayefsky Laurel Award for Television Writing Achievement.

2016 *The Catch* airs; wins International Emmy Founder Award.

Chapter Notes

Chapter 1. "What Am I Afraid They Will See?"

1. "Shonda Rhimes '91 Delivers Dartmouth's Commencement Speech," Youtube video, https://www.youtube.com/watch?v=EuHQ6TH60_I (accessed November 28, 2016).

2. Harold L. Erickson, "American Broadcasting Company (ABC)," *Encyclopedia Britannica,* May 14, 2012, https://www.britannica.com/topic/American-Broadcasting-Company (accessed November 29, 2016).

3. "Career Profiles: Showrunner," *Get in Media*, http://getinmedia.com/careers/showrunner (accessed November 29, 2016).

4. Shonda Rhimes, *Year of Yes* (New York, NY: Simon & Schuster, 2015), p. 97.

Chapter 2. Making Stuff Up

1. "Shonda Lynn Rhimes–Television Producer," top100people.club, http://top100people.club/shonda-lynn-rhimes/ (accessed November 2, 2016).

2. Larry A. McClellan, "University Park", *The Encyclopedia of Chicago*, http://www.encyclopedia.chicagohistory.org/pages/1291.html.

3. Shonda Rhimes, *Year of Yes* (New York, NY: Simon & Schuster, 2015), pp. 2-3.

4. Ibid., p. 19.

5. Shonda Rhimes, "My Life in Books," redbookmag.com, March 18, 2013, http://www.redbookmag.com/life/money-career/interviews/a14941/shonda-rhimes-interview-on-books/ (accessed November 9 2016).

6. Rhimes, *Year of Yes*, p. xiv.

7. Marian Catholic High School website, "About the Band," https://www.marianchs.com/band/about-the-band.php (accessed November 3, 2016).

8. "Year of Yes–Shonda Rhimes Bio," litlovers.com, (updated July 22, 2016), http://www.litlovers.com/reading-guides/14-non-fiction/10724-year-of-yes-rhimes?start=1 (accessed October 21, 2016).

9. Rhimes, *Year of Yes*, p. 97.

10. Oprah website homepage, http://www.oprah.com/index.html (accessed November 2, 2016).

11. "Alumni Profile–Shonda Rhimes," *USC Trojan Family Magazine*, Winter 2005, http://www.usc.edu/dept/pubrel/trojan_family/winter05/rhimes.html (accessed November 8, 2016).

12. Sarah Springer, "Celebrities Talk about Their Most Influential Teachers," *CNN Schools of Thought Blog*, May 11, 2012, http://schoolsofthought.blogs.cnn.com/2012/05/11/celebrities-talk-about-their-most-influential-teachers/ (accessed November 8, 2016).

Chapter 3. The Pursuit of Passion

1. Stacey Wilson Hunt, "'Grey's Anatomy's' Shonda Rhimes Turns Up the Heat in New Series 'Scandal'," *Hollywood Reporter*, June 26, 2011, http://www.hollywoodreporter.com/news/greys-anatomys-shonda-rhimes-turns-205721?utm_source=feedburner&utm_medium=feed&utm_campaign=Feed%3A+thr%2Fnews+%28The+Hollywood+Reporter+-+Top+Stories%29 (accessed November 4, 2016).

2. Dartmouth College website, "Black Underground Theatre Association (BUTA)," (last updated March 31, 2016), http://dgd.dartmouth.edu/group/407 (accessed November 4, 2016).

3. Nelly Mendoza-Mendoza, "Acclaimed Alumni in Pop Culture," *Dartmouth*, April 19, 2016, http://www.thedartmouth.com/article/2016/04/acclaimed-alumni-in-pop-culture (accessed November 4, 2016).

4. Shonda Rhimes, *Year of Yes* (New York, NY: Simon & Schuster, 2015), p. 81.

5. "A Success Story:Shonda Rhimes," bbetterdaily.com, October 13, 2014, http://www.bbetterdaily.com/bbetterdaily-a-success-story-shonda-rhimes/ (accessed November 5, 2016).

6. Hunt, "'Grey's Anatomy's' Shonda Rhimes Turns Up the Heat in New Series 'Scandal.'"

7. "Shonda Rhimes Biography," Internet Movie Database, http://www.imdb.com/name/nm0722274/bio (accessed November 4, 2016).

8. Jessica Cariaga,"USC, NYU Top THR Film School Rankings Again," indiewire.com, July 30, 2015, http://www.indiewire.com/2015/07/usc-nyu-top-thr-film-school-rankings-again-59831/ (accessed November 6, 2016).

9. University of Southern California website, "Did You Know," http://about.usc.edu/facts/did-you-know/ (accessed November 6, 2016).

10. Princeton University: Lewis Centre Arts website, September 30, 2016, "Film and Television Producer Debra Martin Chase at Princeton University," http://arts.princeton.edu/news/2016/09/film-television-producer-debra-martin-chase-princeton-university/ (accessed November 5, 2016).

11. "Year of Yes–Shonda Rhimes Bio," litlovers.com, (updated July 22, 2016), http://www.litlovers.com/reading-guides/14-non-fiction/10724-year-of-yes-rhimes?start=1 (accessed November 5, 2016).

12. "Grey's Anatomy Creator to Receive Mary Pickford Award," USC News press release, May 6, 2009, http://cinema.usc.edu/assets/051/10645.pdf (accessed November 5, 2016).

Chapter 4. The House That Britney Built

1. "Shonda Rhimes," hollywood.com, http://www.hollywood.com/celebrities/shonda-rhimes-57530087/ (accessed November 8, 2016).

2. "Hank Aaron: Chasing the Dream/ Awards," Internet Movie Database, http://www.imdb.com/title/tt0113254/awards?ref_=tt_awd (accessed November 29, 2016).

3. "Hank Aaron," baseballhall.org, http://baseballhall. org/hof/aaron-hank.

4. Stacey Wilson Hunt, "'Grey's Anatomy's' Shonda Rhimes Turns Up the Heat in New Series 'Scandal,'" *Hollywood Reporter*, June 26, 2011, http://www.hollywoodreporter.com/news/greys-anatomys-shonda-rhimes-turns-205721?utm_source=feedburner&utm_medium=feed&utm_campaign=Feed%3A+thr%2Fnews+%28The+Hollywood+Reporter+-+Top+Stories%29 (accessed November 5, 2016).

5. "Halle Berry," biography.com, http://www. biography.com/people/halle-berry-9542339#early-film-career (accessed November 7, 2016).

6. Shonda Rhimes, *Year of Yes* (New York, NY: Simon & Schuster, 2015), p. 78.

7. Hunt, "'Grey's Anatomy's' Shonda Rhimes Turns Up the Heat in New Series 'Scandal.'"

8. "Shonda Rhimes," hollywood.com, http:// www.hollywood.com/celebrities/shonda-rhimes-57530087/ (accessed November 8, 2016).

Chapter 5. "I'd Rather Have a Stubborn Girl"

1. "Oprah Winfrey Network, SuperSoul Sunday," Youtube video, https://www.youtube.com/watch?v=URehJMHN6hI (accessed November 8, 2016).

2. Stacey Wilson Hunt, "'Grey's Anatomy's' Shonda Rhimes Turns Up the Heat in New Series 'Scandal,'" *Hollywood Reporter*, June 26, 2011,

http://www.hollywoodreporter.com/news/greys-anatomys-shonda-rhimes-turns-205721?utm_source=feedburner&utm_medium=feed&utm_campaign=Feed%3A+thr%2Fnews+%28The+Hollywood+Reporter+-+Top+Stories%29 (accessed November 9, 2016).

3. "Article: September 11, 2001," scholastic.com, http://www.scholastic.com/teachers/article/september-11-2001 (accessed November 9, 2016).

4. Susan J. Boutwell, "Shonda Rhimes '91: Insight and Inspiration from a TV Icon," Dartmouth News, June 7, 2014, https://news.dartmouth.edu/news/2014/06/shonda-rhimes-91-insight-and-inspiration-tv-icon (accessed. November 8, 2016).

5. Derrick Bryson Taylor, "Shonda Rhimes Adopts 2nd Baby Girl," essence.com, April 7, 2012, http://www.essence.com/2012/04/07/shonda-rhimes-adopts-2nd-baby-girl (accessed. November 9, 2016).

6. Shonda Rhimes, "Learning to Surrender—Shonda Rhimes: How Adoption Changed Me," *Daily Beast*, April 25, 2013, http://www.thedailybeast.com/witw/articles/2013/04/25/shonda-rhimes-how-adopting-helped-me-learn-to-surrender.html (accessed November 10, 2016).

7. Shonda Rhimes, *Year of Yes* (New York, NY: Simon & Schuster, 2015), p. 8.

8. Rhimes, "Learning to Surrender—Shonda Rhimes: How Adoption Changed Me."

9. Rhimes, *Year of Yes*, p. 8.

10. Taylor, "Shonda Rhimes Adopts 2nd Baby Girl."

11. Rhimes, "Learning to Surrender—Shonda Rhimes: How Adoption Changed Me."

12. Shonda Rhimes, whosay.com, http://www.whosay.com/status/shondaland/736244 (accessed November 9, 2016).

13. "Types of Surrogacy," surrogacyuk.org, https://www.surrogacyuk.org/about_us/types-of-surrogacy (accessed November 10, 2016).

14. Rhimes, *Year of Yes*, pp. 67-69.

15. Ibid.

16. Ibid.

17. Rhimes, *Year of Yes*, p. 10.

18. "Shonda Rhimes on Raising 'Stubborn,' Confident Daughters: 'I Don't Want to Have a Nice Girl,'" *People*, August 17, 2016, http://celebritybabies.people.com/2016/08/17/shonda-rhimes-raising-stubborn-daughters-good-housekeeping/ (accessed November 10, 2016).

19. *Glamour* magazine website, News & Politics section, glamour.com, November 4 2007, http://www.glamour.com/story/shonda-rhimes (accessed November 10, 2016).

Chapter 6. Shaping ShondaLand

1. Colleen Leahey, "The Smartest Question Shonda Rhimes Ever Asked," *Fortune*, September 25, 2014, http://fortune.com/2014/09/25/shonda-rhimes/ (accessed November 11, 2016).

2. "Alumni Profile–Shonda Rhimes," *USC Trojan Family*, Winter 2005, http://www.usc.edu/dept/pubrel/trojan_family/winter05/rhimes.html (accessed November 12, 2016).

3. "How Katherine Heigl Stung Shonda Rhimes: Oprah's Next Chapter: Oprah Winfrey Network," Youtube video, https://www.youtube.com/watch?v=13zAtXwNemE (accessed November 12, 2016).

4. David Hinckley, "'Grey's Anatomy' Creator Shonda Rhimes Is Not Afraid to Pull the Plug on Problematic Actors," NYdailynews.com, April 24, 2015, http://www.nydailynews.com/entertainment/tv/shonda-rhimes-not-afraid-pull-plug-problematic-actors-article-1.2197595 (accessed November 11, 2016).

5. Stacey Wilson Hunt, "'Grey's Anatomy's' Shonda Rhimes Turns Up the Heat in New Series 'Scandal'," *Hollywood Reporter*, June 26, 2011, http://www.hollywoodreporter.com/news/greys-anatomys-shonda-rhimes-turns-205721?utm_source=feedburner&utm_medium=feed&utm_campaign=Feed%3A+thr%2Fnews+%28The+Hollywood+Reporter+-+Top+Stories%29 (accessed November 4, 2016).

6. "Grey's Anatomy," abc.go.com, http://abc.go.com/shows/greys-anatomy (accessed November 5, 2016).

7. "Year of Yes–Shonda Rhimes Bio," litlovers.com, (updated July 22, 2016), http://www.litlovers.com/reading-guides/14-non-fiction/10724-year-of-yes-rhimes?start=1 (accessed November 5, 2016).

8. "Strike over, Hollywood Writers Head Back to Work," CNN.com, February 13, 2008, https://web. archive.org/web/20080413003541/http://www.cnn. com/2008/SHOWBIZ/TV/02/13/writers.strike/ index.html (accessed November 11, 2016).

9. "Oprah's *Next Chapter* Interview," Youtube video, https://www.youtube.com/watch?v=13zAtXwNemE (accessed November 11, 2016).

10. Neely Tucker, "D.C. Insider Judy Smith Is Basis for ABC Drama 'Scandal,'" *Washington Post*, March 30, 2012, https://www.washingtonpost.com/ entertainment/tv/dc-insider-judy-smith-is-basis-for-abc-drama-scandal/2012/03/29/gIQAbT8JlS_ story.html (accessed November 12, 2016).

11. "Oprah's *Next Chapter* Interview," Youtube video, https://www.youtube.com/watch?v=13zAtXwNemE (accessed November 11, 2016).

12. "About Judy," judysmith.com, http://www. judysmith.com/aboutJudySmith.php (accessed November 12, 2016).

13. Shonda Rhimes, *Year of Yes* (New York, NY: Simon & Schuster, 2015), pp. 67-69.

14. Nellie Andreeva, "ABC Buys Legal Thriller from Shondaland & 'Grey's Anatomy' Writer," deadline.com, August 19, 2013, http://deadline. com/2013/08/abc-buys-legal-thriller-from-shondaland-greys-anatomy-writer-567157/ (accessed November 13, 2016).

15. Rick Porter, "ABC Winter/Spring 2016 Premieres: 'The Family' to Sundays, Long Breaks for 'Scandal,'

'OUAT,'" screenertv.com, November 16, 2015, http://tvbythenumbers.zap2it.com/more-tv-news/abc-winterspring-2016-premieres-the-family-to-sundays-long-breaks-for-scandal-ouat/ (accessed November 13, 2016).

16. Yvonne Villarreal, "TV Preview: For Shonda Rhimes, a TV Empire Built on High Drama," *LA Times*, September 12, 2014, http://www.latimes.com/entertainment/tv/sneaks/la-et-st-tv-preview-shonda-rhimes-20140914-story.html (accessed November 14, 2016).

17. Sarah Ball, "What You Should Know About Shonda Rhimes: A Panoply of Eccentric Biographical Data Re: TV's First Lady of Network Drama," *Vanity Fair*, September 2013, http://www.vanityfair.com/culture/2013/09/shonda-rhimes-scandal-memories (accessed November 16, 2016).

18. Nicole Crozier, "Shonda Rhimes on Being Competitive," thisyearone.com, April 24, 2015, http://www.thisisyearone.com/shonda-rhimes-on-being-competitive/ (accessed November 14, 2016).

19. Rhimes, *Year of Yes* (New York, NY: Simon & Schuster, 2015), p. 80

Chapter 7. First. Only. Different

1. Shonda Rhimes, *Year of Yes* (New York, NY: Simon & Schuster, 2015), pp. 136–138.

2. Ibid.

3. Ibid.

4. Rhimes, *Year of Yes*, pp. 138–139.

5. "Shonda Rhimes on Running 3 Hit Shows and the Limits of Network TV," npr.org, November 11, 2015, http://www.npr.org/2015/11/11/455594842/ shonda-rhimes-on-running-three-hit-shows-and-the-limits-of-network-tv (accessed November 16, 2016).

6. "Oprah's *Next Chapter* Interview," Youtube video, https://www.youtube.com/watch?v=13zAtXwNemE (accessed November 11, 2016).

7. Rhimes, *Year of Yes*, p. 70.

8. Juju Chang and Lauren Effron, "Shonda Rhimes Opens Up about Overcoming Shyness, Weight Loss and Her Journey to 'Year of Yes,'" abcnews. com, November 9, 2015, http://abcnews.go.com/ Entertainment/shonda-rhimes-opens-overcoming-shyness-weight-loss-journey/story?id=35033049 (accessed November 15, 2016).

9. Rhimes, *Year of Yes*, p. 141–143.

10. Ibid.

11. Ibid.

12. Ibid, p. 156.

13. Maureen Ryan, "Shonda Rhimes, Creator of 'Grey's Anatomy' and a Chicagoan of the Year," I, December 21, 2005, http://featuresblogs. chicagotribune.com/entertainment_tv/2005/12/ shonda_rhimes_a.html (accessed November 18, 2016).

14. "Golden Globes 2007: Greys Anatomy Best TV Drama," Youtube video, https://www.youtube.com/

watch?v=dfnaR7kPWvM (accessed November 21, 2016).

15. *Glamour* magazine website, News & Politics section, glamour.com, November 4 2007, http://www.glamour.com/story/shonda-rhimes (accessed November 18, 2016).

16. "USC Mary Pickford Alumni Awards," marypickford.org, http://marypickford.org/education/usc-mary-pickford-foundation-alumni-awards/ (accessed November 5, 2016).

17. "Shonda Rhimes Accepts Golden Gate Award at the GLAAD Awards," Youtube video, https://www.youtube.com/watch?v=iHp2WvspFfs (accessed, November 20).

18. "Shonda Rhimes," curtisbrown.co.uk, https://www.curtisbrown.co.uk/client/shonda-rhimes (accessed November 21, 2016).

19. "Tony Goldwyn Presents Founders Award to Shonda Rhimes," Youtube video, https://www.youtube.com/watch?v=DpKpBC0k_-A (accessed November 20, 2016).

20. "Shonda Rhimes to Receive Norman Lear Award," womenandhollywood.com, http://womenandhollywood.com/shonda-rhimes-to-receive-pgas-2016-norman-lear-award/ (accessed November 21, 2016).

Chapter 8. "You Are Not Alone"

1. "Shonda Rhimes' Human Rights Campaign Speech: Top Ten Most Inspirational Quotes,"

hollywoodreporter.com, March 16, 2015, http://www.hollywoodreporter.com/news/shonda-rhimes-human-rights-campaign-781669.

2. Ibid.

3. Ibid.

4. Willa Paskin, "Network TV Is Broken. So How Does Shonda Rhimes Keep Making Hits?," *New York Times*, May 9, 2013, http://www.nytimes.com/2013/05/12/magazine/shonda-rhimes.html (accessed November 21, 2016).

5. Ibid.

6. *Glamour* magazine website, News & Politics section, glamour.com, November 4, 2007, http://www.glamour.com/story/shonda-rhimes (accessed November 18, 2016).

7. "Quote of the Day: Shonda Rhimes "I Make TV Look Like the World Looks," womenandhollywood.com, http://womenandhollywood.com/shonda-rhimes-to-receive-pgas-2016-norman-lear-award/ (accessed November 21, 2016).

8. "GLAAD History and Highlights," glaad.org, http://www.glaad.org/about/history (accessed November 21, 2016).

9. Paskin, "Network TV Is Broken."

10. "Shonda Rhimes Accepts Golden Gate Award at the GLAAD Awards," Youtube video, https://www.youtube.com/watch?v=iHp2WvspFfs (accessed November 20).

11. Shonda Rhimes, *Year of Yes* (New York, NY: Simon & Schuster, 2015), pp. 138–139.

12. Kim Quindlen, "27 Lessons about Living Your Fullest Life, from Shonda Rhimes in Her New Book 'Year Of Yes,'" thoughtcatalog.com, January 11, 2016, http://thoughtcatalog.com/kim-quindlen/2016/01/27-lessons-about-living-your-fullest-life-from-shonda-rhimes-in-her-new-book-year-of-yes/ (accessed November 18, 2016).

Chapter 9. "Don't Call Me Lucky"

1. Willa Paskin, "Network TV Is Broken. So How Does Shonda Rhimes Keep Making Hits?," *New York Times*, May 9, 2013, http://www.nytimes.com/2013/05/12/magazine/shonda-rhimes.html (accessed, November 21, 2016).

2. "Alumni Profile–Shonda Rhimes," *USC Trojan Family*, Winter 2005 issue, http://www.usc.edu/dept/pubrel/trojan_family/winter05/rhimes.html (accessed November 12, 2016).

3. Shonda Rhimes, *Year of Yes* (New York, NY: Simon & Schuster, 2015), p. 55.

4. Ibid.

5. Rhimes, *Year of Yes*, p. 57.

6. Sarah Ball, "What You Should Know about Shonda Rhimes: A Panoply of Eccentric Biographical Data Re: TV's First Lady of Network Drama," *Vanity Fair*, September 2013, http://www.vanityfair.com/culture/2013/09/shonda-rhimes-scandal-memories (accessed November 16, 2016).

7. Shonda Rhimes, "My Life in Books," redbookmag. com, March 18, 2013, http://www.redbookmag. com/life/money-career/interviews/a14941/shonda-rhimes-interview-on-books/ (accessed November 20 2016).

8. Ted Johnson, "Shondaland Stars Headline New Hillary Clinton Ad," *Variety*, March 10, 2016, http:// variety.com/2016/biz/news/hillary-clinton-scandal-kerry-washington-shonda-rhimes-1201727835/ (accessed November 22, 2016).

9. Natasha Singh, "Shonda Rhimes Talks Politics and the Upcoming Season of 'Scandal,'" abcnews. com, March 17, 2016, http://abcnews.go.com/ Entertainment/shonda-rhimes-talks-politics-upcoming-season-scandal/story?id=37706727.

10. Ashley Lee, "Shonda Rhimes Stresses Importance of Diverse TV in Trump Era: 'My Pen Has Power,'" *Hollywood Reporter*, November 21, 2016, http:// www.hollywoodreporter.com/news/shonda-rhimes-stresses-diverse-tv-trump-era-international-emmys-2016 (accessed November 21, 2016).

11. "How Katherine Heigl Stung Shonda Rhimes: Oprah's Next Chapter: Oprah Winfrey Network," Youtube video, https://www.youtube.com/ watch?v=13zAtXwNemE (accessed November 2, 2016).

12. Juju Chang and Lauren Effron, "Shonda Rhimes Opens Up about Overcoming Shyness, Weight Loss and Her Journey to 'Year of Yes,'" abcnews. com, November 9, 2015, http://abcnews.go.com/ Entertainment/shonda-rhimes-opens-overcoming-

shyness-weight-loss-journey/story?id=35033049 (accessed November 15, 2016).

13. "Shonda Rhimes '91 Delivers Dartmouth's Commencement Speech," Youtube video, https:// www.youtube.com/watch?v=EuHQ6TH60_I (accessed November 28, 2016).

Glossary

academic A teacher or scholar from a university or institute of higher education.

accolade An award.

advocate A person who publicly supports or recommends a particular cause or policy.

affinity A natural liking or feeling of empathy for something or someone.

agent A person who is authorized to act for or in the place of another.

aptitude A natural ability to do something.

avid Showing great enthusiasm for or interest in something.

binge watching The practice of watching multiple episodes of a television program in a short space of time.

biopic A biographical film.

caesarean section A surgical operation for delivering a child through the mother's abdomen.

cliche An overused or obvious expression, lacking in originality.

commencement A graduation ceremony.

condescending Treating someone as if you are more important or more intelligent than them.

diversity Exhibiting a variety, such as relating to race, gender, ethnicity, or sexuality.

documentary A nonfiction film.

esteemed Respected and admired.

ethnicity Belonging to a group that shares a cultural tradition.

euphoric Feeling intense excitement and happiness.

fellowship An academic award or aid.

feminist A person who supports feminism.

F.O.D. Stands for "First. Only. Different." A phrase that refers to barrier breakers.

genetically Related by genes.

hijack To illegally seize a vehicle while in transit and force it to go to a different destination.

homophobic An irrational aversion to, or discrimination against, homosexuality or homosexuals.

introvert A shy person who does not reveal thoughts or feelings readily.

Ivy League An elite group of colleges and universities in the United States, known for their exclusivity and academic rigor.

LGBTQ An abbreviation for "lesbian, gay, bisexual, transgender, and queer."

media mogul A successful entrepreneur or businessperson who owns and controls any media-related company or enterprise.

memoir A collection of personal stories or memories from one's life.

producer A person responsible for the financial or managerial tasks involved in putting on a show.

rosary A form of prayer used in the Catholic Church, often while holding a string of beads, also called a rosary.

ShondaLand The production company founded by Shonda Rhimes, which has been behind television shows such as *Grey's Anatomy*, *How to Get Away with Murder*, and *Scandal*.

showrunnner The executive producer who oversees all of the scripts, character development, and writing and directing staff of a television show.

spin-off A television show that derives, or "spins off," from another television show.

surrogacy The process of giving birth as a surrogate mother or of arranging such a birth.

thesis A long essay or project written by a candidate for a university degree.

trailblazing Making or leading toward a new way.

war correspondents Journalists who report from a scene of war.

Further Reading

Books

Landau, Neil. *The TV Showrunner's Roadmap: 21 Navigational Tips for Screenwriters to Create and Sustain a Hit TV Series*. New York, NY: Focal Press, Taylor and Francis Group, 2014.

Rhimes, Shonda. *Year of Yes*. New York, NY: Simon & Schuster, 2015.

Roberts, Emily. *Express Yourself: A Teen Girl's Guide to Speaking Up and Being Who You Are* (The Instant Help Solutions Series). Oakland, CA: Instant Help, 2015.

Websites

Get in Media

www.getinmedia.com

Get in Media provides information about career options in all areas of the media industry, including film and television. The website offers company profiles, job descriptions, and interviews with media professionals to help you understand the career options within the entertainment business.

Teen Ink

www.teenink.com

Teen Ink is a national teen magazine, book series, and website that publishes submissions from students aged thirteen to nineteen. It accepts creative work in the form of writing, art, and photography and has been running for twenty-five years.

Index